MILITARFAHRZEUGE
by
WALTER J. SPIELBERGER

PASSENGER CARS

Before the first World War, the mechanization of the German Army progressed at a most modest pace. The automobile, barely capable of standing on its own, was not too well suited for the rigors of a military application. October 1, 1899, saw the first introduction of motor vehicles during the "Kaiser" maneuvers. During World War I, civilian passenger cars in increasing numbers were being used for many a purpose, while motorcycles and so-called "Kleinautos" made themselves useful for messenger services. The "grosse Personenkraftwagen" saw service with open superstructures for the transport of staff officers, while enclosed specialized bodies enabled these vehicles to work as ammunition carriers, workshop units, radio/communication vans and especially as ambulances.

A multitude of types and variations were available, complicating the makeshift maintenance and spare parts organizations, as type restriction and standardization was never contemplated during this time, nor would it have been feasible. The end of the war returned many of these vehicles to civilian use. The truck industry, expanded far beyond normal capacities by the demands of war, saw itself forced to switch also to passenger car production, and as a result, by 1924, 65 German manufacturers were building as many as ninety different types of passenger cars. In a country which neither had the resources nor the financial capacity to sustain such an industry, economic conditions during this time reduced the total of automotive companies to 23 by 1928.

During this time, the Reichswehr, the new German Army, made some feeble attempts to develop passenger cars for military use. Since individual Army commands were made responsible for the procurement of these vehicles, whose numbers were by necessity very limited; only standard, off the line commercial passenger car chassis were available. They received open bodies, called "Kuebelsitzer" and were typical for their time.

1925/26 also saw the first attempt to create a special cross-country passenger vehicle for military purposes. With three axles, these units had either four driven rear wheels, or, as in the case of the Selve vehicle, a 6x6 configuration. Daimler-Benz and the Horch factory of Zwickau participated in producing prototypes which were soon found to be too expensive for mass production. Krupp of Essen finally brought this development to a conclusion in building the so-called "Krupp-Baersch" 6x4, a vehicle which was equally well suited as a passenger car and a light truck. Renamed type "L 2 H 43" or "Krupp-Protze", this model was introduced in substantial numbers with Wehrmacht units after 1933.

January of 1930 saw the conclusion of trials with commercial passenger car chassis mounting open four-seater bodies with canvas tops and side curtains to protect the crews against adverse weather.

Most of these vehicles received larger tires and a modified rear axle ratio. With the beginning of 1937, the side curtains were gradually replaced by sheet metal doors, but cross-country ability of these units left much to be desired. Originally only the types "Stuttgart 260" of Daimler-Benz and "Favorit" of Adler were considered for this purpose.

As a smaller unit, the BMW-Dixi chassis was purchased in numbers, to serve as a messenger vehicle, Hanomag delivering their type "4/23 PS" in this category. Attempts to mount machine guns on these vehicles were made to provide anti-aircraft protection for mechanized formations. Both the BMW and the Adler "Favorit" chassis were destined to receive lightly armored superstructures. The conversion of the Adler vehicle resulted in the creation of the Kfz. 13 and 14. (See Volume 5).

Hitler's takeover in 1933 brought an attempt to classify the existing vehicles and the following categories were established:

light motorcycle	cylinder displacement up to 350 cc
medium motorcycle	cylinder displacement up to 500 cc
heavy motorcycles	cylinder displacement above 500 cc
light passenger car	cylinder displacement up to 1500 cc
medium passenger car	cylinder displacement above 1500 cc
heavy passenger car	cylinder displacement above 3000 cc

These categories held true for chassis identification only, while the superstructures were classified according to their use. Thus, the following army vehicles, based upon commercial passenger car chassis, were in inventory by 1935:

with the chassis of the light passenger car
      light cross-country passenger car (Kfz. 1)
      light radio-communications car (Kfz. 2)
      tank dummy

with the chassis of the medium passenger car
      medium cross-country passenger car (Kfz. 11)
      medium cross-country passenger car with trailer hitch (Kfz. 12)
      communication vehicle (Kfz. 15)
      medium survey section instrument carrier (Kfz. 16)
      radio communication vehicle (Kfz. 16)
      weapons carrier (Kfz. 18)

with the chassis of the heavy passenger car
      Only standard commercial vehicles with standard production bodies were used in this category, mainly for the transportation of staff officers.

The light chassis received on a later date, three additional special superstructures for the following purposes:
      radio vehicle (Kfz. 2)
      maintenance vehicle (Kfz. 2/40)
      light survey section instrument carrier (Kfz. 3)

The capacity of individual firms was never sufficient to meet the demand of the expanded armed forces of Germany during this time. Again, a large variety of different models was added to the inventory, a disadvantage which was especially felt during the war. The main suppliers of passenger cars to the Wehrmacht were:
    Adler-Werke AG.: Favorit (1929-33), Standard 6 (1930-34) 3 Gd (1938-39)
    Auto-Union AG.:
    Werk Horch: 830 (1933-35), 830 B (1933-35), 830 BK (1935-38)
    Werk Wanderer: W 11 (1928-32), W 23 S (1937-39), W 24 (1937-40)
    BMW AG.: 3/15 (1928-31), 303 (1933-34), 320 (1937-38), 326 (1936-41)
    Daimler-Benz AG.: 260 (1928-32), 170 (1931-35), 200 (1933-36) 170 V (1936-42), 290 (1936-37), 320 (1936-40)
    Hanomag AG.: 3/16 (1928-30), 4/23 (1931-35), Kurier (1934-38), Rekord (1934-38)

In place of the heavy passenger car chassis, light trucks were used until 1935. Only Daimler-Benz created a replacement chassis for the former 6x4 passenger cars, namely the type "G 4". A vehicle widely known, because Hitler used it frequently during his visits to front troops. Both Horch and Krupp made

ARMOR SERIES   VOL.10

MILITARFAHRZEUGE

German Softskinned Vehicles of WW2

by
Walter J. Spielberger
and
Uwe Feist

ISBN-0-8168-2036-8

Aero Publishers, Inc.

329 Aviation Road
Fallbrook, California 92028

© **AERO PUBLISHERS, INC.**

1970

Library of Congress Catalog Card Number

68-31782

We wish to express our appreciation to Col. Robert J. Icks, USAR — Retired, for his assistance rendered in compiling Armor Series Vol. 9 "Sonderpanzer" and this Volume.

Photo Credits:

    Col. R. J. Icks

    Bundesarchiv-Militararchiv

    R. P. Hunnicutt

    Bart Vanderveen

Editor's note: Because the original German specifications and terms used in this book are based on the metric system, the following table is included for convenient referral.

unit	abbreviation	approximate U.S. equivalent
1 centimeter	cm	0.39 inches
1 kilogram	kg	2.2046 pounds
1 kilopond	kp	2.2046 pounds (not affected by atmospheric pressure)
1 kilometer	km	0.62 miles
1 liter	ltr	1.057 quarts liquid
1 metric ton	t	1.1 tons
1 millimeter	mm	0.04 inches

Cover Painting: Daimler-Benz Medium cross country truck type L 3000 A

Printed and Published in the United States of America by Aero Publishers, Inc.

similar attempts but built prototypes only. 1934 saw first attempts to create standard army passenger cars, the so-called "Einheits Personenkraftwagen." Designed by the Ordnance Department, they were to be built by different manufacturers according to standard plans. Three categories were envisioned:

1. standard chassis for light passenger car (two versions with different trackwidth)
2. standard chassis for medium passenger car (one version only)
3. standard chassis for heavy passenger car (two versions, one with front, the other with rear engine)

Suspension components for all vehicles were identical, as standardization was attempted on a large scale. All vehicles, with the exception of the medium chassis, were equipped with four-wheel steering. All models had four-wheel drive.

It was soon found to be impossible to also develop suitable uniform power plants for these vehicles, and it was left to the manufacturers to install appropriate engines coming off their own production lines. This arrangement further complicated the already strained spare parts system and brought about many an unpleasant surprise during field repairs.

Bayerische Motorenwerke AG. of Eisenach started to build the first version of the light chassis in 1938 and installed its six-cylinder "325" power plant. At the same time, Hanomag of Hannover equipped its version with a four-cylinder "20-B" engine. Last but not least, Stoewer of Stettin participated in the production of these vehicles and built five different models from 1937 through 1940. All companies involved produced a simplified version, called type "40", by the end of 1939. These vehicles had the four-wheel steering eliminated. They remained in production until 1943.

They replaced in many instances the commercial chassis in operation and received the same superstructures as previously mentioned under the light chassis classifications. In addition, an "anti-aircraft vehicle" (Kfz. 4), was issued to motorized infantry units, mounting two machine guns 34 in a pivot with 360° traverse.

The medium chassis, appearing in 1937, was exclusively built by the Horch factory of the Auto-Union concern. "V" 8 engines were standard for most models, with the exception of a substantial number of vehicles which were equipped with the Opel 3.6 litres six-cylinder power plant. 1940 saw the introduction of a simplified version, which stayed in production until 1943. A large number of special bodies were used on this chassis, which now gradually replaced the commercial chassis of former years. Some of the units were fitted with convertible bodies for the use by high staff officers.

The chassis I for the heavy passenger car was intended to be used exclusively for the light armored car. It had a 3.5 litre Horch engine installed in the rear. Mechanical brakes were provided. An improved version, the Ausf. "V", was built from 1941 to 1943, and came equipped with the 3.8 litre Horch V 8 engine. Hydraulic brakes were now installed. The production of the heavy chassis II, a conventional layout, with front engine, started relatively late, toward the end of 1938. Auto-Union produced the types "Ia" and "Ib", both with the 3.8 litre Horch engine. "Ia" had four-wheel steering, while "Ib" had only the front wheels affected. A subsidiary of the German Ford factory in Berlin participated in this model run and created three models of the heavy passenger car chassis. All were equipped with the Ford 3.6 litre V 8 engine. Auto-Union continued in 1940 with the type "40", a simplified version, mounting either the Horch or the Ford power plant. Production was stopped in 1941. The use of these chassis was identical to the one of the light trucks. With special bodies, they were used among others as:

Telephone-communication vehicles (Kfz. 23)
Relay vehicle (Kfz. 24)
Ambulance (Kfz. 31)
Prime mover vehicle (Kfz. 69)

Weapons carrier (Kfz. 70)
Light anti-aircraft vehicle (Kfz. 81)
Light searchlight vehicle I and II (Kfz. 85)

An armored version of the chassis was called "heavy, armored passenger car" (Sd. Kfz. 247). Anti-air-craft formations of both Luftwaffe and Army received limited numbers of a self-propelled 2 cm anti-aircraft weapon.

The "Einheits" chassis, as interesting as its development was, was too complicated and demanded too many man hours af far as production and maintenance was concerned. They proved to be too heavy and limited in payload capacity. Their total number expressed in production figures was not overwhelming and 1941 saw the termination of their production after the "Schell-Program" had been approved.

Daimler-Benz, left out in the development and production of the "Einheits" vehicles, created a very similar vehicle of its own, the type "G 5". Equipped with four wheel drive and steering, they found their way to some army units, while others were issued to mountain rescue outfits. A total of 320 units were produced. A few years earlier, the same company had developed another cross-country passenger car, the rear-engined "160 H". Only three prototypes were produced. An interesting development took place at the Tempowerke in Hamburg. During 1938, this company built and sold a unique cross-country passen-ger car, the type "G 1200". With two two-cycle engines, one in front and one in rear, and four-wheel drive, either engine and wheel drive components could be used separately. The Army was obviously not interested in this design. The development of amphibious vehicles for the German Army was never pursued with much enthusiasm. Private initiative generated by a certain Mr. Trippel started produc-tion on a small scale. Approximately 1,000 units of his type "SG 4" were produced by 1944, when pro-duction ceased. A number of prototypes, including armored and amphibious reconnaissance and supply vehicles, appeared over the years but never went into production.

Briefly to mention, but difficult to incorporate within the framework of this publication, are the numerous products of the German motorcycle industry. Because of its far above average production capacities, a large number of them found their way into German Army units. The climax in the development of Army motorcycles came in 1940, when both BMW and Zuendapp created their heavy 750ccm vehicles, with drive to the side cars. Russia soon rendered them useless as both road and weather conditions pointed out the shortcomings of their basic design.

On November 1, 1941, the man in charge of motorization for the Reich, General Schell, reported to Hitler that of all the 55 different types of passenger cars produced before the war, only one was to be retained in production. This lone survivor was the Volkswagen. It assumed the functions of the light passenger car chassis, both commercial and "Einheits", while chassis of the newly created 1.5 ton truck series replaced both the medium and heavy passenger car chassis.

The basic Volkswagen design, appearing on Professor Porsche's drawing boards as early as 1935, in-cluded by 1936 a cross-country vehicle. Called type "62" and built only in few prototype vehicles, it had the normal VW layout. An open body and larger tires did not give the unit the desired off-road capabil-ities. When the decision was reached in 1940 that the Volkswagen was going to be the only passenger car of the German armed forces, a re-design was initiated, resulting in the type "82" with increased ground clearance and reduction gears on the rear axle to enhance traction and mobility. Starting in March of 1943, a larger power plant with 1131 ccm was installed. A total of approximately 55,000 units was produced by the end of the war. Assembly took place at the Volkswagen factory in Wolfsburg, while the open bodies came from the Ambi-Budd factory in Berlin. Four-wheel drive versions were investigated but soon dropped again, since the basic simplicity of the type "82" fitted right into the economical situation of war-time Germany. Nevertheless, 1942 saw the introduction of an amphibious version of the Volks-wagen the Porsche type "166". With shorter wheel base, larger tires, four-wheel drive and a screw for propulsion in water, this vehicle was to replace the sidecar motorcycles in German motorized formations. A total of 14,265 units was completed by 1944, when production was stopped, due to raw material shortages and damages to production sites.

In summing up the development of military passenger cars for the German Army, it should be emphas-ized that it stood quite frequently throughout the years in the shadow of other more pressing production programs. The "Einheits" program, the only attempt to create specialized vehicles, suffered under too comprehensive a program resulting in too complicated a vehicle with too many variations. These mis-takes were soon realized and opened the door in 1940 for the production of only one multi-purpose vehicle, the Volkswagen. Most other Armies followed this example rather quickly and even today most countries possess only one vehicle of this kind for their military forces.

The motorcycle industry in Germany, one of the most predominant in the world, supplied a substantial number of these vehicles to the Army. They were used mainly for messenger duties but also served for many other purposes.

Concluding the development of heavy military motorcycles was this BMW "R 75", a special design which incorporated a drive to the sidecar.

Its counterpart was the Zuendapp "KS 750" of almost identical dimensions. Both vehicles were issued to "Kradschuetzen" units where they served until they were replaced in part by the amphibious Volkswagen.

As early as 1927, the BMW factory, after taking over the Dixi-Werke in Eisenach, built, under license, the British Austin "Seven" passenger car. Some of them were used within the Reichswehr as light passenger cars but also as tank "dummies". Attempts were made to arm some of these vehicles with machine guns for anti-aircraft protection purposes.

Hanomag's light 1.1 litre passenger car, built from 1932 to 1934, was converted into a three-seater military vehicle and officially called "leichter gelaendegaengiger Personenkraftwagen" (Kfz. 1).

A different version, using the same Hanomag chassis, was used as a small telephone communication vehicle with the designation "Kfz. 2".

Medium passenger car chassis, equipped with open military superstructures, were built by various manufacturers. Picture shows Daimler-Benz, Adler and Wanderer vehicles during instruction classes in negotiating difficult terrain.

The Adler "Favorit" chassis, in production from 1925 to 1929, served not just with military, but also with police units. A few of these vehicles received armored super-structures.

The Wanderer "W 11" chassis, in turn, served as medium cross-country passenger car (Kfz. 11) or when equipped with a trailer hitch, as Kfz. 12. It was typical, as an example for military vehicles of this time.

The same Wanderer vehicle in somewhat modified appearance as "Kfz. 12" with canvas roof in position and with side curtains provided for weather protection.

The Daimler-Benz "200", was one of the most numerous representative in its class. Larger tires and a modified drive axle ratio were the only basic differences with the commercial passenger car chassis.

A weapons carrier version, using the same Mercedes-Benz chassis, served as prime mover for light, anti-tank guns or the light infantry howitzer. They also towed an ammunition trailer. Its nomenclature was "Gefechtskraftwagen" (Kfz. 18).

Auto-Union supplied, among others, their famous Horch chassis within this category. Their type "830 B1" appeared as communication vehicle "Kfz. 15", equipped with a V 8 engine. Picture shows the vehicle during a parade with top and side curtains in open position.

The same vehicle with complete weather protection in place. During winter time, this so-called protection proved to be most inadequate.

With enclosed bodies, some of these vehicles served as radio communication vans, called "Kleinfunkkraftwagen" (Kfz. 17).

Most of the enclosed bodies produced during this time were made of wood. Note the large tires mounted on these vehicles to increase the payload capacity.

Toward the end of the model run the vehicles received sheet metal doors and removable side windows. Chassis type is a Daimler-Benz "230", a well-known passenger car.

This "Kfz. 12", its trailer hitch clearly indicated, was used in anti-tank formations to tow the 37 mm gun. Windshield could be folded forward.

The larger version of the Daimler-Benz "320", equipped with a 3.4 litre engine, also received its military counterpart. Used as "Kfz. 15", the large wheel base of this vehicle was not always conducive in negotiating difficult terrain.

Some of the many captured vehicles, sometimes available in substantial numbers, were modified to receive standard German Army superstructures. Typical of such a modification is this British Morris "C 8" commercial chassis fitted with a "Kfz. 15" body.

The German Army also used consistently regular commercial chassis fitted with a variety of superstructures. Picture shows a Protos "C 1" vehicle used as an ambulance. They served military installations during peace time.

The smallest of the so-called "Einheits" vehicles was a light vehicle built by several manufacturers. Picture shows the Stoewer version, equipped with a 2 litre engine. All these vehicles had originally four wheel drive and four wheel steering.

The BMW version was identical in its appearance but had a BMW six-cylinder engine installed. These vehicles replaced to a large extent the commercial chassis procured during previous years.

An anti-aircraft version, the "Kfz. 4", mounted two MG 34's in a tripod with 360° traverse. They were to protect motorized infantry from low-flying enemy planes.

The medium "Einheits" chassis, built exclusively by Auto-Union, came also with a variety of different superstructures. This unit is leading a "Kradschuetzen" outfit, infantry on motorcycles, with an older Wanderer vehicle next to it.

They were most prominent with armored and motorized Infantry units, replacing the former commercial passenger car chassis.

They could be found in Africa, like this unit with members of the Afrika Korps. The open version carried up to five passengers. Luggage stowage, however, was severely restricted.

The same vehicle was also issued to Luftwaffe units and received, after 1943, the sand-beige paint of all German Army vehicles. Late versions had the side spare wheel moved to the inside of the superstructure.

Here an aircraft crew is ferried to its plane. Note the "WL" license plate, identifying the unit as an air force vehicle. Different model runs could not be identified from the outside. Neither was the powerplant openly indicated.

An interesting picture shows a propaganda unit in Russia using "Einheits" vehicles with civilian license plates. The superstructure is of unusual design and appears to be a special body for the use of psychological warfare units.

With enclosed bodies, the units served to a large extent as radio communication vehicles. Note the radio antenna on top of the vehicle. Unit is followed by a larger communication vehicle, mounted on a 3 ton Opel truck chassis.

Air force radio vehicles somewhere in France. Note the collapsable antenna and windshield which could be opened. Bodies were made of wood, which was sometimes covered with sheet metal.

A Funkkraftwagen (Kfz. 17) in operation. Note the extended radio antenna which is wire-supported. Antenna was permanently mounted on the rear of the vehicle.

Concluding the series of "Einheits" passenger cars of the Wehrmacht was the so-called heavy type. Here it is shown as a troop carrier with the "Hermann Goring" division. If weather allowed, the windshield was normally lowered and the canvas roof folded down. One MG 34 is mounted for anti-aircraft purposes.

A Flak unit ready to be shipped to Africa is using the heavy passenger car as "leichter Flakkraftwagen (Kfz. 81). They are employed as prime movers for the 2 cm Flak 30.

The final version, the type "40", had the four-wheel steering omitted and the spare wheel mounted inside. Both changes were incorporated mainly to save on production man hours.

DAIMLER-BENZ light cross-country truck type "G 3a"

VOLKSWAGEN light passenger car (Porsche type 82)

FEIST 4

OPEL "BLITZ"   Medium cross-country truck type "3.6 - 6700 Type A"

Feist 70

Trippel of Molsheim made one of the very few attempts to create an amphibious passenger car for the German Army. Several prototypes resulted finally in a small series of production vehicles which were mainly used by SS units.

Vidal of Hamburg created this twin-engined vehicle with four-wheel drive and steering. A number of them were exported to different countries but the German Army was not interested.

A limited number of the heavy p cars served as self-propelled the 2 cm Flak 30. They w to Luftwaffe units in o motorized colu bombers. pro

ere attemp ainst Allied ction for the

Daimler-Benz's type "G 5" was a private enterprise of this company to create a counterpart to the "Einheits" vehicles. Almost identical in its appearance, only a few of these passenger cars were issued to Army units.

They were equipped with four-wheel drive and four-wheel steering and were able to negotiate most difficult terrain. A number of these units were purchased by the German mountain patrol to rescue stranded mountaineers, in inaccessible areas.

Typical of the contribution of foreign manufacturers to the motorization of the German Army was this Austrian "Steyr" type 250. The burning need for additional vehicles forced the Germans to avail themselves of all possible sources. When production facilities were also available, the spare parts problem could still be mastered, but it turned out to be a completely different story the moment captured vehicles of overseas manufacturers were involved.

This BMW "335", built from 1939 to 1940, was one of the most luxurious passenger cars produced in Germany. During the war, it served as means of transportation for high ranking officers.

A typical column of German motor transports. Note not even two of the vehicles are of similar make. Civilian vehicles are mixed with early Army vehicles and "Einheits" passenger cars. A nightmare for a maintenance man. Leading vehicle is an Opel "Admiral", the largest passenger car this General Motors subsidiary built before the war.

During the battle in France in 1940, the staff of an armored corps moves to a new location. While the Commanding General rides in a "540 K" Mercedes, the rest of the staff follows in assorted vehicles of all descriptions.

Four-wheel drive passenger cars for General Officers were built by various companies. This Horch "V 8" was procured in very limited numbers only by the Wehrmacht. Its nomenclature: Schwerer gelaendegaengiger Personenkraftwagen (Kfz. 21).

Hitler's personal choice was this Daimler-Benz "G 4", a 6 x 4 vehicle intended for Party and Army officials. Only one of these vehicles is still in existence today.

A very rare modification of the above unit was the communication vehicle, which allowed for radio contact with headquarters during Hitler's field trips.

A formation of the division "Grossdeutschland" on its way toward a new assignment. This version of the Volkswagen served in many a capacity. Only the rear wheels were driven.

The only passenger car remaining in production during the war was the military version of the Volkswagen. Known as type "82", it served as the standard light passenger car of the Wehrmacht. Vehicles following are 3 ton half-track tractors of the latest version. They had a conventional truck flatbed mounted, instead of the customary enclosed superstructure.

Built for the first time in 1940, the vehicle used standard Volkswagen components and originally a 985 ccm powerplant. Since Waffenamt demanded for all military vehicles an output of at least 25 BHP, its displacement was increased to 1131 cc.

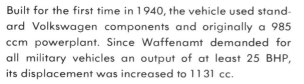

Built as inexpensively as possible, the vehicle utilized easy to build body components. A reduction gear mounted on the ends of the rear axle shafts and its light weight allowed for the same cross-country mobility as its four-wheel driven predecessors.

Everything was simple on its basic design. Accessibility to the engine was good. After initial difficulties, the air-cooled engine soon became one of the most reliable power plants in automotive history.

All other chassis components, especially its torsion bar suspension, are still in production today after millions of Volkswagens have been sold throughout the world.

Economical and dependable, the Volkswagen served the German armed forces in all capacities. Picture shows a Luftwaffe crew utilizing its services.

Used in Africa under most difficult conditions, they soon established an outstanding reputation. Special sand tires were fitted in this theatre of war and captured vehicles were one of the most sought-after booty for Allied troops.

The amphibious version, the Porsche type "166", was originally intended to replace the many sidecar motorcycles, in Army inventory. Equipped with four-wheel drive and a screw for water propulsion, the vehicle was inventoried as "leichter Personenkraftwagen" (Kfz. 1/20). Vehicles in background are self-propelled 15 cm guns, called "Hummel".

Entering water was no problem for these vehicles. By means of a hook, the propeller was lowered and engaged. Note muffler on top of engine compartment. Steering in water was by front wheels.

Vehicle afloat during exercise. Note windshield and top are lowered. Unit could negotiate all lakes and streams encountered in Western Europe. Maintenance, however, was much more complicated than on the standard version.

It soon became obvious that the amphibious qualities of the vehicles were in no relation to the high amount of man hours required to produce these vehicles. Wartime conditions did not allow for the luxury to continue their production. Production stopped in 1944, after 14,265 units had been produced.

TRUCKS

Load carrying, self-propelled vehicles with internal combustion engines were first ordered by the War Department in October of 1900. The Daimler Motoren Gesellschaft of Cannstadt received an order for eight vehicles which formed the nucleus for a generation of Army trucks. Developments before the war were intended mainly to refine vehicle components in an attempt to make them more reliable. The first vehicles, and the ones which were to follow during the First World War, were basically trucks designed for civilian purposes and consumption. Only minor modifications prepared them for military application. The same situation prevailed when the Reichswehr was formed in 1920. Because of the large variety of vehicles, both civilian and military, used by the German armed forces, a payload classification system was established which should also assist the reader in finding his way through the maze of German army trucks.

A. TRUCKS UP TO 2 TON PAYLOAD

Up to 1938, mostly commercial vehicles were purchased by the Army. Rarely was such a vehicle modified for its specific role and only special superstructures identified them as Army vehicles. They all appeared with the typical 4x2 layout. One of the most popular was the Phaenomen "Granit" with its air-cooled engine, built from 1929 through 1939. Known mainly as an ambulance, "Krankenkraftwagen" (Kfz. 31), it appeared, however, also with a passenger car body of the open style, the so-called "Kuebelwagen". It has already been mentioned that the truck chassis of this payload class ran parallel in designation and usage to the chassis of the heavy passenger car.

These commercial chassis proved unacceptable to the Army in regard to their cross-country ability and they were mainly relegated to supply and training tasks. In June of 1929, the Waffenamt had published specifications for specialized 6x4 trucks with a payload capacity of 1.5 ton on paved roads and one ton off-road. The industry embarked immediately on this project, having anticipated this development for years. Already in 1928, Daimler-Benz had introduced their type "G 3," followed in 1929 by an improved version, the "G 3 a". More than 2000 of these vehicles were built when production ceased in 1934. With open or closed bodies, they served a multitude of purposes, identified always by their specific "Kfz" number. The second company participating in the production of these vehicles was the Buessing-NAG of Braunschweig. Its type "G 31" was in production from 1933 to 1935, during which time 2300 of these units were built. All of the vehicles, regardless of manufacturer, were equipped with gasoline engines, but several prototypes appeared over the years, fitted with Diesel engines. Third in line to produce these trucks was the C. D. Magirus factory of Ulm. Its type "M 206" was built from 1934 to 1937 and also received all the superstructures of the other models. Last but not least, concluding this development, was the Krupp product which was to become the most numerous of them all. Developed as "Krupp-Baersch Wagen", it received in 1933 the designation "L 2 H 43", until a modified version, the "L 2 H 143" appeared in 1936. Both models had an air-cooled four opposed cylinder power plant under a slanting hood, making these units easily recognizable. The power plant, by the way, was almost identical to the one installed in the Panzer I. A diesel engine version also existed. The first three models of this 6x4 production run, namely the Daimler-Benz, Buessing-NAG and Magirus vehicles, served as a basis for the first 6x4 armored cars of the German Army. The Krupp version also had its armored counterpart. While the first three models showed a rather conventional layout the Krupp vehicle with its independent suspension in the rear pointed toward future developments. The multitude of vehicles in this class alone further illustrates the most difficult maintenance situation encountered later during the war. Obviously, the influence of the very powerful automotive industry disregarded to a large degree the needs of the Army. Production of these vehicles had ceased once the units had received their allocated number of trucks. Replacement was provided in the form of vehicles utilizing the heavy "Einheits" passenger car chassis. 1939 saw the German Army entering Poland with a vast conglomeration of vehicles, many of them based upon the afore-mentioned 6x4 units. Since they were already out of production, new ways had to be found to provide replacement vehicles.

A new program, designed to streamline automobile production, was instigated as early as 1938. This so-called "Schell-Programm" controlled the needs of both the military and the civilian vehicle production. Thereby, the Army did forgo their own designs, such as special 6x4 or "Einheits" chassis, in favor of some basic vehicles which could be utilized by the Army, industry and civilians alike. These so-called "Schell" types, built in different payload classes, always appeared in two versions, namely an "S" type with a 4x2 configuration for civilian use, and supply purposes, while its 4x4 counterpart, the "A" type, went exclusively to the armed forces. The vehicle, intended to replace all previous vehicles in the up to 2 ton class, was the type "1500". Daimler-Benz's participation resulted in modifying its former type 1500, which was produced from 1937 to 1941. The improved version, called "1500 S" or "1500 A", depending on its drive train configuration, was kept in production until 1943. The "S" version came mainly equipped with enclosed "fire-fighting" bodies, being issued to many a fire fighting unit. The "A" version with its four-wheel drive, appeared with open bodies with many Army units. Phaenomen of Zittau created a similar vehicle, maintaining its reputation as ambulance manufacturer in fitting most of its "S" type vehicles with ambulance bodies. In addition, radio communication vehicles appeared with this chassis. The open-bodied "A" version was produced in limited quantity only and some of them appeared with sand tires and special air filters for their air-cooled engines. They were designed for use in North Africa, but this campaign was over before they were ready. Auto-Union of Zwickau, the major manufacturer of the former "Einheits" chassis, also got into the act and created a 1.5 ton vehicle. Only prototypes of both the "S" and "A" version were built, when it was decided that they were to produce, under license, the vehicle developed by the Steyr-Daimler-Puch AG. This company did not bother to build an "S" version but embarked exclusively on the production of vehicles for the Army. Equipped with an air-cooled V 8 engine, these vehicles were kept in production until after the war and Steyr alone built 12,450 of these units. They appeared as regular trucks, as ambulances, as weapon carriers and also with a convertible body as a staff vehicle. Updated to a payload of 2 tons during the closing stages of the war, they were kept in production in Austria until 1946. An interesting study shows this vehicle with large steel wheels in an attempt to create a so-called "Ostschlepper." Production figures for vehicles of this load class, according to an official "Speer" report, indicate a total of 66,322 units to be produced between 1941 and 1944.

One of the most numerous standard light trucks in use with German forces was this Phaenomen ambulance. Picture shows one of the early versions with an open driver compartment.

Later production models had the driver cab enclosed but remained otherwise unchanged. They served for many a year with armed forces from their first action in Spain, to the end of the war in 1945.

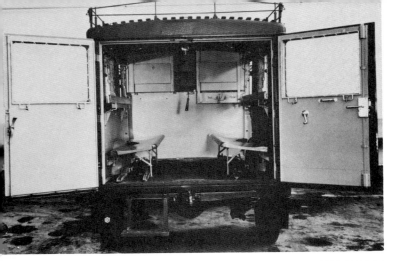

Having a payload of 1.5 metric tons, they carried up to four litter patients. Their cross-country ability left much to be desired.

One of the pre-war commercial one ton trucks, used in numbers by the Wehrmacht, was this Borgward "B1000" vehicle.

One of the "Schell-Programm" models within the 1.5 ton configuration was this Daimler-Benz "L 1500 S". Used mainly in a 4 x 2 version as fire engine, it incorporated all features of the standardized "S" vehicles.

Its 4 x 4 counterpart, the "A" type, served as transportation for staff officers and as prime mover for the 2 cm Flak.

The troop carrier version provided seats for eight. Storage of spare wheels was provided inside of body. Rifle holders are on both sides of the passenger compartment.

The Steyr version of the 1.5 ton model run came in three basic versions. As a truck, it was used as troop carrier, supply vehicle and prime mover for light guns. The elaborate driver cab was later on replaced by a rather primitive cardboard version.

A command car version fitted the transportation needs of high ranking staff officers. Some of these vehicles had bullet-proof glass and reinforced sheet metal doors. All vehicles of the Steyr series had four-wheel drive.

Last but not least, the regular troop version served many a purpose. A "V 8" air-cooled engine propelled all these vehicles.

B. TRUCKS WITH MORE THAN 2 TON AND UP TO 3.5 TON PAYLOAD

Immediately following World War I, only commercial type vehicles were procured by the Army. The development of 6 x 4 trucks in the light vehicle class was, therefore, amended to also create load-carrying vehicles with a payload capacity of 3 tons on paved roads and 2 tons under off-road conditions. Krupp of Essen was one of the first ones to embark on this project and built in 1930 the type "L 3 H 63," which was to become later the type "L 3 H 163". These vehicles remained in production until 1938. Available with either gasoline or Diesel engines, they came equipped with a variety of bodies. Buessing-NAG of Braunschweig appeared on the market in 1933 with their type "III GL 6," a relatively heavy vehicle which was built in limited numbers only. Approximately 300 units were produced.

They were succeeded in 1936 by the type "KD" of which a total of 415 units was produced. These vehicles were built in the Berlin factory of Buessing. Daimler-Benz participation in this model run brought the type "LG 3000" or "LG 63" as it was internally called. In production from 1934 to 1936, a total of 7,434 units were built. Again gasoline and Diesel engines were made available. Most of these vehicles came equipped with a powerful winch with a towing capacity of 3.5 tons, and most of the vehicles could extricate themselves once they got stuck. Main contributor in the supply of these vehicles, however, was the Henschel company of Kassel.

As early as 1928, they produced the type "33 B 1," a 6 x 4 vehicle equipped with a 65 HP four-cylinder engine. At the same time, a six-cylinder model, the type "33 D," went into production. Its Diesel counterpart, the type "33 G 1," was kept in production from 1934 through 1941. It was one of the most typical military vehicles of its time. The success of the "33G1," was such that the Magirus factory in Ulm was asked in 1938 to build this vehicle under license. Identical in its appearance, Magirus, however, installed its own six-cylinder Diesel engine.

Independent from the activities of the manufacturers, the Ordnance Department had developed a vehicle of its own. Called the "Einheitsdiesel," it had a 6 x 6 configuration with independent front and rear suspension. Several manufacturers, among them Buessing-NAG, Daimler-Benz, MAN and Borgward, participated in the production of these vehicles. Kaemper, Henschel, Magirus and MAN were engaged in the production of the six-cylinder 85 HP power plant, a Diesel engine. With various bodies, this type "HWA 526 D" was issued in numbers to many outfits. Its production run was from 1937 to 1940.

An interesting development took place between 1934 and 1936 at the Daimler-Benz Factory. Apart from the afore-mentioned 6 x 4 vehicles, this company investigated the incorporation of independent suspension components on off-road vehicles. 4 x 4, 6 x 6, and 8 x 8 configurations were tried and actual prototypes built. The type "LG 65/2" was the smallest and the few prototypes were later on converted into mountain busses for the German Post Office. Two versions of the 6 x 6 vehicle were built, the types "LG 65/3" and "LG 4000," or as it was internally called, the "LG 68." 150 units of the "LG 65/3" were delivered to the Greek Army, while 70 units of the "LG 4000" found their way to various military establishments. The eight-wheeled version, the type "LG 65/4," appeared in only a few prototype vehicles.

The "Schell-Programm" of 1938 eliminated all these vehicles and replaced them during 1940 with "S" and "A" type trucks of the newly-designed 3 ton series.

With very few changes, Daimler-Benz appeared in 1940 on the market with their type "L 3000 S" and in 1941 with its four-wheel drive counterpart, the type "L 3000 A." The bulk of the 3 ton vehicles, however, came from the newly-established Brandenburg factory of the Adam Opel AG., a subsidiary of General Motors. Their type "3.6-36 S 3 t" or "Blitz" was started in production in 1938 and continued to the end of the war. In 1943, Daimler-Benz phased out its own designs in order to participate in the production of the Opel "S" type. Opel's "A" version, the type "3.6-6700 A," was built from 1940 through 1944. At least 100 different bodies were officially recorded, mounted on these vehicles. Kloeckner-Humboldt-Deutz (former Magirus) built mainly their "A" version, the type "A 3000," equipped with a four-cylinder Diesel engine. All "S" type vehicles, with their wheel base enlarged, could also be fitted with bus bodies. Borgward of Bremen started in 1942 with their models and built the types "B 3000 S/O," "B 3000 A/O" and "B 3000 S or A/D" until the end of the war. Another main contributor within the 3 ton class was the German Ford company of Cologne. All their vehicles, "S" type trucks only, came equipped with either four or eight cylinder gasoline engines. Their type "V 3000 S" was retained in production after Germany's surrender in 1945.

One of the most numerous and most typical of German military vehicles during the Thirties was this Krupp "Boxer". A vehicle with a 6 x 4 configuration, it was the most prominent within the series developed in 1929. Picture shows the troop carrier version, the Mannschaftkraftwagen (Kfz. 70) during a parade.

Equipped with an air-cooled four-cylinder opposed powerplant, the vehicles served well during the initial phases of World War II.

As "Protzkraftwagen" (Kfz. 69), it was used as prime mover for the 37 mm anti-tank gun, as well as for the 75 mm light infantry howitzer. It also pulled an ammunition trailer. Gun crew and ammunition was carried on the vehicle.

Note the arrangement of the spare wheel between the two rear seats. Foot rests are provided for two gun crew members on this prime mover version.

A Flak unit during a parade in 1938. As "leichter Flakkraftwagen" (Kfz. 81), the unit towed the 2 cm Flak 30.

Several police formations utilized this vehicle as a squad car. A different version was intended for the use by high ranking government officials. Even armored versions existed of this vehicle.

Next to participate in this model run was the "G 31" model built by Buessing-NAG. A standard truck with 6 x 4 drive train layout, it served in the same capacity as the aforementioned Krupp vehicle.

The Magirus version within the same model run was the type "M 206". All these vehicles were available to civilian consumers, making it possible to produce larger quantities at decreased prices.

Daimler-Benz's participation in the motorization of the German Army was diversified and highly interesting. They incorporated, among others, independent wheel arrangements for 4 x 4, 6 x 6 and 8 x 8 cross-country vehicles. Picture shows the smallest model of this development, the type "LG 65/2".

Their conventional model with a regular 6 x 4 configuration was the type "G 3" and its improved version the "G 3 a".

Daimler-Benz with its employment of independent suspension units created military vehicles of outstanding cross-country ability. Picture shows front wheel drive configuration on the 6 x 6 version. To further increase their mobility, some of the vehicles had rollers mounted in front and rear to assist in negotiating difficult terrain. This is the Daimler-Benz type "LG 4000".

Within the 3 ton class, various manufacturers again participated to create almost identical vehicles. Daimler-Benz built this 6 x 4 version called "LG 3000", which was available either with gasoline or Diesel engines. This is an Air Force vehicle, called "Flakmesstruppkraftwagen" (Kfz. 74).

Army units used these vehicles for engineering and signal corps formations. Most of these trucks had a winch installed in front of the radiator.

The Henschel version, the type "33 G 1" was one of the most numerous 6 x 4 vehicles within the 3 ton series. It was also built under license by the Kloeckner-Humboldt-Deutz AG and served among others as prime mover for the 88 mm Flak.

Engineering outfits towed their pontoons with these vehicles. Windshield and canvas top could be lowered to facilitate loading and storage.

The Krupp 3 ton 6 x 4 version was another entry into this field. It was allocated with open and closed superstructures and saw action in almost all theatres of war. It was finally replaced by the "Schell" A-type vehicles.

Road conditions in Russia normally ranged from bad to worse. If it was not dust, it was bottomless mud which hampered the movements of German supply columns.

Picture above shows Magirus trucks of a supply unit, picture below points out the fact that even four-wheel drive Opel vehicles got stuck on roads like these.

Many a different body appeared on the Krupp "L 3 H 63" chassis, like this "Befehlskraftwagen" (Kfz. 72). It was used as a command center for staff officers. Its total weight was 6.4 metric tons.

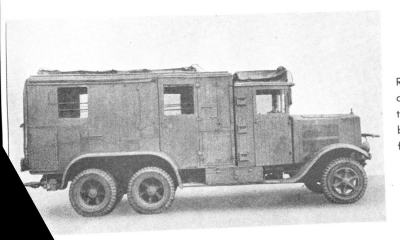

Radio communications were most vital for the conduct of armored warfare. Thus, all armored formations received a number of "Funkkraftwagen" based upon the 3 ton chassis. They were to connect field forces with their headquarters.

Buessing's "III GL 6" was one
to build a 6 x 4 cross-cou
to be too heavy, but it
the "Reichswehr" tir
hicle houses a prin

The "Einheitsdiesel" was to replace all previous 3 ton 6 x 4 vehicles. It had all six wheels driven and came equipped with a standardized six cylinder 85 BHP Diesel engine. Various manufacturers produced this vehicle.

Propaganda units used these vehicles for transmittal of news from the battle front. This vehicle, still bearing a civilian license plate, is protected by a Panzer IV.

Artillery units employed this vehicle as flash detection equipment carrier. Note the wooden superstructure, typical for most German vehicles of this era. Its official nomenclature was "Lichtauswertekraftwagen" (Kfz. 62).

Commercial trucks of all load classes found their way into the German armed forces. They served as supply vehicles in many outfits and had still to be used during the war. This is a MAN 3-ton truck used as "mittlerer Lastkraftwagen" for telephone line construction.

Other commercial chassis received specialized superstructures like this Magirus "1 C V 100" truck being equipped as a mobile radio station.

The "Schell" program stipulated a 3 ton load class with two basic vehicle configurations. The "S" type having a 4 x 2 arrangement, while the "A" type came equipped with four-wheel drive. Borgward participated in this model run with their type "B 3000 S/O". The vehicle was available with gasoline or Diesel engines. Its four-wheel drive counterpart had the designation "B 3000 A".

Kloeckner-Humboldt-Deutz build a similar vehicle with a type number "A 3000". The "S" version was mainly used for fire engines.

Daimler-Benz brought both types to the market, an "A" version, called "L 3000 A" and its 4 x 2 counterpart, the "L 3000 S". Both vehicles saw extensive service within the German armed forces.

Diesel powered vehicles were favored in Russia, since the vehicle's radius of action was greatly increased. Vehicle belongs to SS outfit operating in the southern part of the Russian front.

The standard enclosed body of the German Wehrmacht fitted on all 3 ton vehicles. It served in at least one hundred official applications. Superstructure was made of pressed cardboard, since wood and sheet metal could no longer be made available for soft-skinned military vehicles.

General Motors Opel factory in Brandenburg was one of the main suppliers of 3 ton vehicles for the German Wehrmacht. Opel "Blitz" vehicles could be seen in all theatres of war and were also built by Daimler-Benz starting in 1944.

Vehicles of an SS outfit carries a twin machine gun 34 for anti-aircraft purposes. Vehicle was equipped with a six-cylinder 3.6 litre powerplant, an original Chevrolet development.

This air force outfit in Russia has made a makeshift self-propelled mount using an Opel vehicle. The 2 cm Flak, normally towed behind the vehicle, is mounted on the flat bed, a very rare modification.

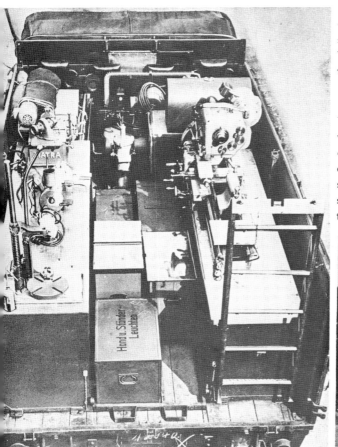

One of the many uses for the 3 ton vehicle was to serve as a mobile workshop for armored formations. This vehicle carries all equipment necessary to maintain and repair armored vehicles.

The four-wheel drive version of the Opel vehicle was the type "3.6-6700 Type A". It remained in production only until 1944 and was considered as one of the most useful vehicles the German Army possessed. It also appeared with numerous superstructures, among others, an ambulance body for the transport of wounded personnel.

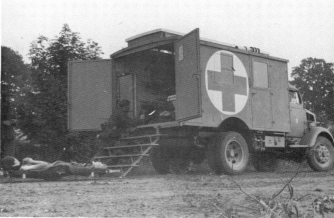

Most of the "S" type vehicles of the 3 ton model run could also be equipped as buses. With an extended wheel base, these vehicles served as normal buses, as mobile offices and as large ambulances. One of specialized body shown in this picture could easily be converted to serve all these purposes.

French trucks, like this Renault "AHN" unit, suffered most under the impossible road conditions in Russia. Yet, a large number of German formations were exclusively equipped with these vehicles.

C. TRUCKS WITH MORE THAN 3.5 TON AND UP TO 5 TON PAYLOAD

Special cross-country vehicles did not appear in this class before the introduction of the "Schell-Programm". Up to this moment, only commercial vehicles were utilized and procured in small numbers. Daimler-Benz participated in this program with their type "L 4500 S" from 1941 on, a type which was also built under license by the Austrian Saurer Werke, starting in 1944. The same two manufacturers produced also an "A" version, the type "L 4500 A". One of the other large manufacturers, engaged in the production of these vehicles, was the Buessing-NAG company of Braunschweig. Their types "500 S" (1939-41) and "500 A" (1940-41) were succeeded by their improved products, the types "4500 S" and "4500 A". Their production was continued after the war. Vehicles for civilian use came factory-equipped with wood-gas generators. The MAN factory of Nuremberg and its subsidiary, the Viennese Oesterreichische Automobil Fabrik, produced their "S" version, the type "SML" until 1946, while the "A" type, called "SMLG," went out of production in 1943. Henschel of Kassel had originally intended to participate in this model run, but their production facilities, however, were used exclusively for tank production. After building some prototypes under the designation "HGS/A 4500, the design was incorporated in 1940 in a joint venture when Henschel, Saurer of Vienna and Kloeckner-Humboldt-Deutz founded a "Development company for trucks". Using the Henschel design as a basis, Saurer produced the majority of the type "BT 4500", while KHD embarked on it on a limited scale, producing mainly fire engines. Used for many purposes and mainly to supply front units, a grand total of 41,970 4.5 ton units were built between 1941 and 1944.

The five-ton load class saw mainly commercial trucks used for military purposes. Tool boxes and other stowage, typical for military vehicles were provided, as were longer running boards to accommodate personnel being transported on these vehicles.

Within the "Schell" program, the 4½ to 5 ton loading class received new members. Here is the Buessing-NAG "A" type vehicle, used mainly for supply purposes within panzer formations. A 4 x 2 version was also available.

These vehicles were subjected to rough going during the winter months in Italy and especially in Russia. Similar versions were built also by MAN and Saurer.

Daimler-Benz again contributed to this model run in supplying both the "A" and the "S" versions. Few of their "A" version vehicles came equipped as self-propelled mounts for the 37 mm Flak. The driver compartment was slightly armored.

D. TRUCKS WITH MORE THAN 5 TON PAYLOAD

The few vehicles of interest in this class appeared toward the end of the war. Up to then, only commercial trucks had been used, very few of them with four-wheel drive. Interesting was an attempt to provide tank formations within the "Schnelle Divisionen" with tank transporters. For the Panzer I, a 4x4 version of the standard 6.5 ton truck built by Buessing-NAG was used. This type "654" was in production from 1936 to 1939. A 6x6 version, the type "900 A", was in existence as prototype only; therefore, the 6x4 version, the type "900", was utilized as a carrier for Panzer II. They normally towed a flat bed trailer, the Sonder Anhaenger 115, with a capacity of 10 tons. Another model, frequently encountered, was the Faun type "L 900 D 567", with a payload capacity of 8800 kp. A modified version with an eight-wheel configuration, the type "L 1500 D 87", was to replace it in 1939. Rapidly increasing tank weights, however, forced the Army to abandon this project.

The need for heavier load-carrying vehicles for the German Army was realized in late 1943, with the introduction of the type "6500/111" produced by Ringhoffer-Tatra of Kolin, Czechoslovakia. A 6.5 ton, 6x6 vehicle with unique features, it never appeared in numbers with German forces. Dr. Ledwinka's famous design with tubular frame and independent front and rear suspension followed a long line of remarkable Tatra vehicles. Equipped with a 12 cylinder, air-cooled, 210 HP engine, this vehicle also had a 8 ton version, the type "8000/111". It was kept in production by the Czechs after the war and was used by both their Army and civilians.

The story of Germany Army transports would not be complete without mentioning the numerous civilian vehicles pressed into service at the beginning of the war. They served their purpose dutifully during the initial stages of the conflict, when road conditions in western Europe were generally acceptable. With the beginning of the Russian campaign, however, their shortcomings were soon revealed, and these deficiencies plagued German units until the end of the war. The contribution of factories in occupied countries was insignificant, since their products were not suited for Russia either. They and the vast number of captured vehicles from all over the world only complicated the already overtaxed German supply system and caused numerous critical situations.

In summary, the multitude of different vehicles in the German Army was always a liability. Production was never sufficient to meet all demands, and the products themselves were mostly of ordinary design. It is a matter of record that Germany's achievements in this area were rather insignificant.

A multitude of civilian vehicles had found their way into the inventory of the German armed forces. The German Reichspost, the postal services of the Reich, was one of the largest automobile fleet owners in the world. Their vehicles, like this Magirus mail van, served army post offices throughout the war.

To supply the German Army, however, large numbers of civilian transports were pressed into service. Maintained partially by Party organizations, like the "Organisation Todt", they brought vital goods to all fighting outfits. Our picture shows a 6.5 ton Buessing-NAG truck of the "650" series, pulling a 5 ton trailer. Triangular sign on top of driver cab indicates that trailer is pulled. Single vehicle would have the indicator in horizontal position.

A tractor, frequently employed by Army and Luftwaffe Units, was this Hanomag "SS 100". Luftwaffe units used it for towing airplanes, bombs and gasoline trailers. It was strictly a commercial tractor which was available in substantial numbers also for civilian use.

The variety of vehicles, used by the German Army is indicated in this picture. Domestic and foreign vehicles were used to make up a supply system which failed all too often because of spare parts supply difficulties. Horse drawn supply columns were retained by the German Army throughout the war.

The bulk of the supply however, was carried by the "Reichsbahn". Everything required for the fighting Front from rifle ammunition to spare engines for fighter aircraft had to be carried over thousands of miles to the various supply depots. The train is pushing two wagons to detonate mines which frequently were placed under the tracks by partisans.

ARMOR SERIES

Each volume of this series consists of 52 pages, including four pages of full color drawings or action paintings of these vehicles. Descriptive text presents a view into the background and history of each vehicle and its development. Over 70 excellent photos, many never before published. Technical data rounds out the total coverage and provides a comprehensive look at that portion of the German armor story. 7½ x 11. Text and photographs by Walter J. Spielberger. Creative art by Uwe Feist. $3.00 (A) each

Vol. 1

THE TIGER TANKS Features all members of the Tiger Tank Family.

Vol. 2

THE GERMAN PANZERS From Mk. I to Mk. V "Panther." All other models of German tanks of the Second World War are covered in this volume.

Vol. 3

STURMARTILLERIE From assault guns to Hunting Panther (Part I) Continues the development of the German armored force; featured are self-propelled guns and tank destroyers.

Vol. 4

STURMARTILLERIE Self-propelled guns and flak tanks (Part II) Concludes the chapter on those vehicles derived from basic tank chassis.

Vol. 5

STRASSENPANZER The full story of German four, six and eight-wheeled armored cars.

Vol. 6

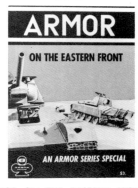

ARMOR ON THE EASTERN FRONT An Armor Series Special Shows German and Russian armored forces in action on the Russian front, 1941-1945. Side view drawings of the German Mark III F, Tiger (P) Elephant, Russian SU 85 and KW I (KVI).

Vol. 7

HALBKETTENFAHRZEUGE. Half tracked vehicles.

Vol. 8

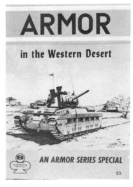

ARMOR IN THE WESTERN DESERT. Another pictorial special, featuring allied and axis armor in action in the North African campaign.

Vol. 9

SONDERPANZER German special purpose and prototype vehicles.